BITCOIN BASICS

A BEGINNER'S GUIDE TO BITCOIN AND BLOCKCHAIN

MARC GORDON

Visit Marc Gordon's author page at Advise Author Publishing.

INTRODUCTION

The fact that you found "Bitcoin Basics" and made a choice to learn more about Bitcoin, blockchain, distributed ledger technology, and the future of value exchange already says a lot.

We are about to begin a journey together that may completely change your attitude towards money; particularly the old kind of money, which is referred to as 'currency' and endlessly issued by governments at whim.

Bitcoin is a new and superior form of digital currency, a medium of exchange and a store of value that operates much differently than standard fiat currencies like the US Dollar, the British Pound and the Japanese Yen.

Here's a quick introduction covering the key facts you need to know about Bitcoin. Where do we begin? Well, first of all, no person, company, or organization is in control of Bitcoin.

This is because it's a decentralized digital currency that's powered by a huge, distributed network of computers.

It uses a type of network referred to as a blockchain. Bitcoin is an asset, and the bitcoin network is a blockchain (a special type of network with unique properties).

The following quote best explains the difference between Bitcoin and a blockchain.

"Blockchain is the tech. Bitcoin is merely the first mainstream manifestation of its potential."

– Marc Kenigsberg

But back to the main point at hand. What needs to be explained before moving forward is the concept of ownership as it relates to Bitcoin. Ownership and having possession of Bitcoin is quite a bit different than having possession of US Dollars or another fiat currency.

In reality, owning a bitcoin simply means having the power and ability to be able to transact with it and send it to someone else. Or you can choose to hold it in your blockchain wallet in hopes that it will appreciate in value.

Bitcoin is superior in many ways to a bank account because each cryptographic bitcoin blockchain wallet contains a private key, a unique encryption style password that allows you to maintain full control over the asset without any third party interference.

Your Bitcoin will be extremely safe as long as you don't share this key with anyone or put it in a place it can easily be found like on your computer, which is connected to the internet or in your email.

When you are the only one who holds the private key to your wallet, it is then only you who has access to your funds.

You can send, receive and store it using a secure digital wallet app, which you can download for free. After creating a Bitcoin wallet, you will have the ability to both send and receive Bitcoin securely.

It's really important to remember that because no bank or other financial intermediary ever has access to your wallet app, you're in charge of keeping it secure.

Bitcoin emerged out of the 2008 global economic crisis when big banks were caught misusing borrowers' money, manipulating the system, and charging exorbitant fees.

To address such issues, Bitcoin creators wanted to put the owners of bitcoins in-charge of the transactions, eliminate the middleman, cut high-interest rates and transaction fees, and make transactions transparent.

They managed to do something revolutionary in creating a distributed network and technology in which people could control their funds in a completely transparent way.

Bitcoin Has Experienced Rapid Growth

Bitcoin has grown rapidly and spread far in a relatively short period of time. Across the world, companies from a large jewelry chain in the U.S., to a private hospital in Poland, now accept bitcoin currency.

Multi-billion dollar corporations such as Dell, PayPal, Microsoft, and Expedia are all dealing in bitcoins.

Websites promote bitcoins, magazines are publishing bitcoin news, and forums are discussing cryptocurrencies and trading in bitcoins.

Bitcoin has its own Application Programming Interface (API), price index, trading exchanges, and exchange rate.

However, there are issues with bitcoins such as hackers breaking into accounts, high volatility of bitcoins, and long transaction delays. Elsewhere, particularly people in third world countries, find Bitcoins as a reliable channel for transacting money, by being able to bypass pesky intermediaries.

Although people refer to bitcoin as a decentralized digital currency, I prefer to think of it as an electronic asset, to sidestep questions around which government backs it and who sets the interest rate, which is often a mental block in understanding bitcoin.

As an electronic asset, you can buy bitcoins, own them, and send them to someone else. Currently (as of April 2020), there are around 18.3 million bitcoins that have been created.

This number will increase by about 25 bitcoins every 10 minutes, with an agreed limit of 21 million, the last of which should be created just before the year 2140.

1

WHAT IS BITCOIN?

Bitcoin was and will always be the **first decentralized digital currency**, also known as a cryptocurrency. It works like cash or gold and it can be transferred on the internet and across the globe in a simple transaction of less than five minutes. With Bitcoin, you can transfer money almost **as easily as sending an email.**

One of the most amazing features about Bitcoin is its ability to send money **person-to-person** without a middleman or involvement of any third party.

In other words, you avoid expensive fees and long waiting times as at the bank and your bitcoin wallet essentially acts as a bank vault, giving you ultimate control over your finances.

Bitcoin was officially created in 2008 by an unknown person or group of people using the name Satoshi Nakamoto.

As such the code behind Bitcoin follows the ideas set out in a whitepaper created by this mysterious and pseudonymous developer Satoshi Nakamoto or a group preferring to use this name as a shield of sorts.

THE THEORY that it may have been made by a group rather than an individual is due to the rough translation of the name:

IN JAPANESE, the name roughly translates into:
Satoshi: clear-thinking, quick-witted, wise
Naka: inside, or relationship
Moto: the foundation

So we can put that together to mean a clear thinking, wise relationship with sound money. The foundation of a new system of value exchange.

Regardless of who is really behind this new technological marvel, the Bitcoin network first came online in 2009 when its source code was released as open-source software.

Bitcoin offers the promise of lower transactional fees when compared to traditional online payment mechanisms and the Bitcoin network is operated by a decentralized authority, unlike government-issued currencies.

There are no physical bitcoins, only balances kept on a public ledger in the cloud, that – along with all Bitcoin transactions – is verified by a massive amount of computing power.

Bitcoins are not issued or backed by any banks

or governments, nor are individual bitcoins valuable as a commodity.

Despite it not being legal tender, Bitcoin charts high on popularity, and has triggered the launch of hundreds of other virtual currencies collectively referred to as Altcoins.

UNDERSTANDING BITCOIN

Bitcoin is commonly referred to as a cryptocurrency, a unique type of digital asset that uses cryptographic code to secure the network, its ledger balances and its transactions. Balances of Bitcoin tokens are kept using public and private "keys," which are long strings of numbers and letters linked through the mathematical encryption algorithm that was used to create them.

The public key (comparable to a bank account number) serves as the address which is published to the world and to which others may send bitcoins.

The private key (comparable to an ATM PIN) is meant to be a guarded secret and only used to authorize Bitcoin transmissions.

Bitcoin keys should not be confused with a Bitcoin wallet, which is a physical or digital device that facilitates the trading of Bitcoin and allows users to track ownership of coins.

The term "wallet" is a bit misleading, as Bitcoin's decentralized nature means that it is never stored "in" a wallet, but rather it exists as a ledger balance on a blockchain.

Style notes: according to the official Bitcoin Foundation, the word "Bitcoin" is capitalized in the context of referring to the entity or concept, whereas "bitcoin" is written in the lower case when referring to a *q*quantity of the currency (e.g. "I traded 20 bitcoin") or the units themselves. The plural form can be either "bitcoin" or "bitcoins." Bitcoin is also commonly abbreviated as "BTC."

. . .

How Bitcoin Works

BITCOIN IS ONE of the first digital currencies to use peer-to-peer technology to facilitate instant payments.

The independent individuals and companies who own the governing computing power and participate in the Bitcoin network, also known as "miners," are motivated by rewards (the release of new bitcoin) and transaction fees paid in bitcoin.

These miners can be thought of as the decentralized authority enforcing the credibility of the Bitcoin network.

New bitcoin is being released to the miners at a

fixed, but periodically declining rate, such that the total supply of bitcoins is constantly inflating but is capped at an upper limit of 21 million.

In this way, Bitcoin (and any cryptocurrency generated through a similar process) operates differently from fiat currency; in centralized banking systems, the currency is released at a rate matching the growth in goods in an attempt to maintain price stability, while a decentralized system like Bitcoin sets the release rate ahead of time and according to an algorithm.

Bitcoin mining is the process by which bitcoins are released into circulation. Generally, mining requires the solving of computationally difficult puzzles in order to discover a new block, which is added to the Blockchain.

In contributing to the Blockchain, mining adds and verifies transaction records across the network. For adding blocks to the Blockchain, miners receive a reward in the form of a few bitcoins; the reward is halved every 210,000 blocks.

In 2009, the reward was 50 new bitcoins divided up amongst the miners involved in operating the network per block. As of 2019, it was 12.5 bitcoins per block and as of May 2020 after the halving it has been reduced to 6.25 BTC per block . As more and more bitcoins are created, the difficulty of the mining process – that is, the amount of computing power involved – increases.

The mining difficulty began at 1.0 with Bitcoin's debut back in 2009; at the end of the year, it was only 1.18. As of October 2019, the mining difficulty is over 12 trillion. Once, an ordinary desktop computer sufficed for the mining process; now, to combat the difficulty level, miners must use expensive, complex hardware like Application-Specific Integrated Circuits (ASIC) and more advanced processing units like Graphic Processing Units (GPUs). These elaborate mining processors are known as "mining rigs."

Another interesting thing to know about Bitcoin is that one bitcoin is divisible to eight decimal places

(100 millionths of one bitcoin), and this smallest unit is referred to as a Satoshi. If necessary, and if the participating miners accept the change, Bitcoin could eventually be made divisible to even more decimal places, giving it an ability to expand like no other currency ever before seen in history.

2

THE HISTORY OF BITCOIN

The path that a revolutionary technology may take is unpredictable to say the least. Take the first ever Bitcoin transaction for example.

It was used to purchase 2 pizzas, for a grand total of 10,000 bitcoin by Hanyecz on May 22nd, 2010.

Today, this transaction has been recorded as the most expensive food order in history at roughly $100,000,000 total or $50,000,000 per pizza.

The date Hanyecz made his purchase, May 22nd, is now termed, "Bitcoin Pizza Day" and is celebrated by cryptocurrency enthusiasts worldwide.

From a pseudonymous programmer and two famous pizzas to the black market and a fan site for a fantasy card game: The world's first cryptocurrency has taken a long and winding road.

Just like a cent is the smallest unit of the United States dollar, a satoshi is the smallest unit of bitcoin. Simply put, it is the smallest denomination with which transactions can be carried out. This unit is referred to as a satoshi to remind people of Satoshi Nakamoto, the originator(s) of Bitcoin.

One of the biggest financial stories of the few past years has been the incredible rise of bitcoin.

The virtual currency was designed to revolutionize peer-to-peer transactions; it doesn't require a go-between (like a bank or credit card network), the exchange of personal information, or transaction fees.

Yet while many are still confused about what exactly a "bitcoin" is and how the nascent cryptocurrency works, just as much confusion exists about where bitcoin came from and how it got to where it is today -- a technological innovation that has shaken the financial world to its core.

A BITCOIN PRIMER on Blockchain

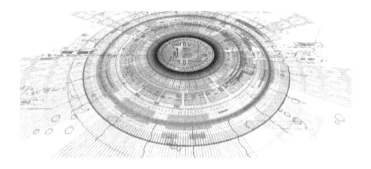

The backbone of bitcoin is the blockchain technology it uses to record the transactions on its network. A blockchain is essentially a publicly distributed ledger; it records each and every bitcoin transaction ever made on a block.

When that block's memory is full, it is added (in sequential order) to the chain of blocks. This ledger -- freely available on any computer in the bitcoin network -- validates bitcoin transactions, stores the Blockchain, and relays transactions to other network computers. These computers are called nodes.

Because the database is stored on a network of

computers, rather than on a single server, hacking or stealing bitcoin data is virtually impossible for would-be cybercriminals.

A hacker would have to break into the majority of nodes simultaneously, a virtually impossible task.

There is also only a predetermined number of bitcoins that can ever be created, meaning that the currency cannot be devalued in the future by a central bank issuing more.

Thanks to the claimed advantages of the cryptocurrency, the only thing that has risen faster than the number of bitcoin enthusiasts is the price of a bitcoin token.

As of May 2020 the price of one bitcoin remains between a range of $8900 to $9200. It had come a long way from its low of $4000 as of Jan. 2020.

If you had bought the low you would have received more than a 100% ROI in less than a single year. Suffice to say timing is everything as Bitcoin is an extremely volatile digital asset.

Satoshi Nakamoto and The Mysterious Origin of Bitcoin

IN LATE 2008, the financial crisis was in full swing. In September of that year, Lehman Brothers Holdings, then the fourth-largest investment bank in the world, filed for Chapter 11 bankruptcy protection.

As the world's financial infrastructure was crumbling, the domain bitcoin.org was registered. Later in 2008, a person or group using the pseudonym Satoshi Nakamoto published a white paper on bitcoin to a cryptography mailing list, explaining how the cryptocurrency would work.

In early 2009, Nakamoto mined the first-ever bitcoin, known as the "genesis block." Embedded in the programming of this first bitcoin was the text

"The Times 03/Jan/2009 Chancellor on the brink of second bailout for banks."

The text refers to a headline on that date from the British newspaper The Times, and is generally seen as proof of the date bitcoin was first mined.

Others also believe it pointed to the crumbling financial infrastructure of the modern world, and the need for a new way forward.

The first bitcoin transaction soon followed when a bitcoin was sent from Nakamoto to Hal Finney, a cryptography expert and enthusiast.

To this day, Satoshi Nakamoto's identity remains a mystery. Several people have claimed to be the mysterious programmer or, as often suspected, a group of programmers; numerous attempts have been made to identify the person or group, but none have been satisfactory enough to be viewed as conclusive.

The only personal details that Nakamoto gave to others were claims to be living in Japan and to have been born on April 5, 1975.

Nakamoto encouraged other cryptographers to assist with the coding, but the creator stepped away from bitcoin in 2011 and has not been publicly seen or heard from since.

As you will soon see, Satoshi Nakamoto is not the only infamous alias in the annals of bitcoin.

FROM PIZZA to the Silk Road

In May 2010, a Florida programmer named Laszlo Hanyecz offered 10,000 bitcoins in exchange for pizza. A British enthusiast took Hanyecz up on the offer and ordered two pizzas to be delivered from a pizza place near Hanyecz's residence; the Briton paid for the pizza using a credit card, and Hanyecz reimbursed the purchase with 10,000 bitcoins.

This is believed to be the first time bitcoin was ever used to make a purchase, and May 22 is celebrated in the bitcoin community as Bitcoin Pizza Day.

What makes the transaction even more memorable, however, is the incredible value the bitcoins used to purchase two pizzas have accrued.

As I write, those bitcoins are worth approximately $90,000,000! But who wants those inflationary US dollars anyway? From the looks of it, having the bitcoin today would be even better.

While the pizza purchase is celebrated, in bitcoin's early days, very few places of business accepted bitcoin as payment.

One area where bitcoin's anonymous nature and digital movement were prized, however, was the black market. It quickly became apparent that bitcoin filled a huge need in the criminal underworld.

In 2011, an online dark-web marketplace dubbed Silk Road was founded by Ross Ulbricht, who ran the site using the pseudonym Dread Pirate Roberts.

The use of Tor routers (so users could browse in anonymity) and untraceable bitcoin payments proved to be a potent combination to avoid detection and arrests by law enforcement.

In founding the site, Dread Pirate Roberts claimed libertarian ideals, saying customers would be free to purchase anything without fear of violence or arrest.

Later, he wrote that he wanted Silk Road "to grow into a force to be reckoned with that can challenge the powers that be and at last give people the option to choose freedom over tyranny."

While his intentions might have been noble, the site freely allowed all sorts of illegal drugs to be bought and sold with impunity.

In October 2014, almost 14,000 product listings on Silk Road were found to be illegal drugs, including cannabis, heroin, LSD, MDMA, and methamphetamine.

Other illegal items like fake driver's licenses could also be purchased, though categories like child pornography and weapons were banned from the site.

Before Ulbricht was found and arrested, Silk Road had over a million active user accounts and had accounted for 1.2 million transactions worth 9.5 million bitcoins. While the price of bitcoin fluctuated wildly during the time of the site's operation, the total was estimated to be worth about $1.2 billion.

An intensive search was conducted by a joint task force that included agents from the FBI, Internal Revenue Service, Drug Enforcement Administration, and U.S. Marshals; they finally found Ulbricht to be the man behind the site and arrested him at a San Francisco public library in October 2013.

While Silk Road was shut down, cryptocurrencies remain popular in black markets, as they offer buyers and sellers a cloak of anonymity without the limitations of using large amounts of cash.

Bitcoin Billionaires

THERE IS a lot to be learned from the price action of Bitcoin over the many years that it has traded as a digital asset and commodity. It has very humble and modest beginnings.

It's hard to imagine that if you had bought Bitcoin in July 2012 you could have acquired them for only $9.35 each. That would be a very good price considering they are worth thousands of times more than that today.

The most recognizable Bitcoin billionaires

would probably be Harvard students Tyler and Cameron Winklevoss: identical twins, Olympic rowers, and long time rivals of Mark Zuckerberg.

After the brothers' fell out of the public spotlight, a spotlight they had entered due to their epic legal battle with Facebook and Zuckerberg himself, some would say that they had given up on their pursuit of changing the world. It would be easy to do considering their epic Facebook idea had been stolen and turned into a multi billion dollar company.

Planning to start careers as venture capitalists, the brothers quickly discover that no one would take their money after their fight with Zuckerberg. While nursing their wounds in Ibiza, they accidentally run into an eccentric character who told them about a brand-new idea: cryptocurrency.

Immersing themselves in what is then an obscure and sometimes sinister world, they begin to realize "crypto" is, in their own words, "either the next big thing or total bulls--t." There was nothing left to do but make a bet or walk away.

"If you have gold, start building up bitcoin reserves," Tyler Winklevoss, who cofounded bitcoin and crypto exchange Gemini with his brother in 2014, told attendees at the Crypto Finance Conference in Switzerland. "We think bitcoin will disrupt gold."

"Once the likes of Tesla's Elon Musk or Amazon's Jeff Bezos start mining gold on asteroids, which will happen within 25 years, gold's value will change," Tyler said, to laughter from the audience, adding that gold investors need to "buy bitcoin."

The fact is that Bitcoin has changed the lives of many if they were so fortunate to understand its power early on and invest in it.

Bitcoin price index from July 2012 to April 2020
(in U.S. dollars)

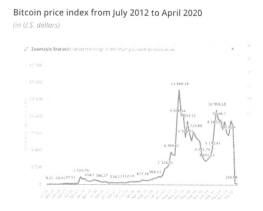

IN MARCH 2013, the total cumulative valuation of all bitcoins in circulation hit $1 billion.

While this was an arbitrary milestone, it was probably not a coincidence that the cryptocurrency soon started attracting the attention of Silicon

Valley and venture capitalists. The best-known of these early investors were the Winklevoss twins themselves.

Cameron and Tyler Winklevoss are probably better known for filing a lawsuit claiming that while they were all students at Harvard University, Facebook founder Mark Zuckerberg stole their idea for the social networking site; they ultimately received a $65 million settlement.

The twins insisted on collecting the lawsuit's settlement in shares of Facebook, not cash. When Facebook went public, the twins used that money to begin amassing a fortune in bitcoin, estimated to be worth approximately $1.3 billion late last year.

The Winklevosses are also majority owners in Gemini, a virtual currency exchange they founded after realizing how difficult it was to buy and sell bitcoin.

Bitcoin's current price may ultimately prove to be in bubble territory. But few of the world's cryptography experts, libertarian dreamers, and successful venture capitalists ever dreamed the cryptocurrency would become what it is today.

For example, when Bitcoin was first created it was almost impossible to think that it would be adopted to the point of having ATM machines dedicated to buying and selling the digital asset using FIAT currencies.

In fact the number of Bitcoin ATMs has exploded over the past few years going from around 1000 machines in 2017 to a staggering 8000 machines in 2020. If that isn't considered mass adoption, I really wouldn't know what is.

But what functionality could you expect from a Bitcoin ATM?

Well, when you see one up close and personal you'd notice that it is not so dissimilar to a standard bank managed ATM. There is an ability to deposit cash and an ability to withdraw cash.

But when using a Bitcoin ATM to deposit FIAT money like US dollars and see it converted you'll need your Bitcoin wallet address so the machine knows where to send the Bitcoin after it makes the currency conversion.

Number of Bitcoin ATMs worldwide from February 2017 to May 2020

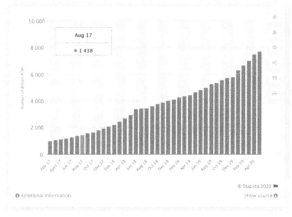

TO SUMMARIZE THIS CHAPTER, it would be appropriate to say that Bitcoin has shocked and amazed the majority of naysayers who firmly stood by their belief that it had no business being a currency. But, obviously the free market has firmly disagreed.

As of 2020, this point is proven by the fact that a single Bitcoin will cost you over $9500. It has also proven its resilience and usefulness as a deflationary asset that easily runs circles in outperforming the king of all FIAT currencies, the mighty US Dollar.

Many also claim that it is a superior form of money to every other alternative on the planet. In future chapters I will discuss just why that may be true.

3

THE DIFFERENCE BETWEEN A BITCOIN WALLET AND A BANK ACCOUNT

W HAT MAKES A BITCOIN WALLET DIFFERENT FROM A BANK ACCOUNT?

A bank account is a financial contract between a client and a bank, through which the balance and all the financial movements of the client (fiat money) are stored and controlled.

A cryptocurrency (Bitcoin) wallet is a software or software hardware solution that can be accessed with keys, both public and private (which always go together). With these keys you can send and receive cryptocurrencies through the Blockchain.

Often wallets are usually compared to bank accounts. Now I'm going to discuss five important differences between a bank account and a Bitcoin wallet:

1.) The Way Currency is Stored

THIS IS perhaps the main difference that allows us to distinguish between a bitcoin blockchain wallet and a bank account.

A blockchain wallet's main functions include the ability to store cryptocurrencies, transfer them and receive them. Many cryptocurrency wallets are able to store and transfer multiple cryptocurrencies such as Bitcoin, Ethereum, Dash, and any other cryptocurrencies that are supported.

On the other hand, bank accounts only allow for safe storage and transfer of fiat money, that is: euros, dollars, and pesos. Furthermore you'll need a separate account for each of those currencies, something that will have to be negotiated and set up with each individual bank based on their service offerings.

2.) Public and Private Keys

IN A WALLET, both the public key and the private key are very large numbers, and generally, their representation is in a separate WIF wallet import format, consisting of numbers and letters.

On the other hand, bank accounts are limited numbers, generally of 20 numerical digits that are divided into groups that identify the bank, the branch, the type of account, and finally, the individual identifier of the client.

3.) Control Over Stored Money

. . .

IN A DIGITAL WALLET, you have absolute control over the cryptocurrencies that are stored, being able to freely carry out any type of transaction without authorization or intervention of third parties and without restrictions of territory (in the case of wallets it is accessed through the private key or public key).

On the other hand, a bank account requires authorization from the bank to carry out certain transactions in addition to restrictions on certain holidays (holidays in general or bank holidays), territories (different countries) and certain limits on daily operations (daily amount, number of transactions, etc.) the movements are made by online banking, checks, credit/debit cards, and window operations in the same bank.

4.) Accessing Money and Security

MOST DIGITAL WALLETS work through websites or applications requiring an internet connection (although the latter is not an indispensable condition due to the appearance of Cold Wallets).

In terms of security, the private key that is stored

in the wallet, it is the only means to access the money registered in a public address (if the private key is lost, the money would also be lost), although the latter may seem to be not very flexible, it offers a high standard of security against third parties. In addition to having higher security protocols due to global standards.

On the other hand, in a bank account, the money is accessed through online banking (which is accessed via the Internet and varies according to each bank) and through credit/debit cards, although these methods may offer more flexibility to the user.

The point against this is that the level of security is lower because online banking depends on the security measures applied to the platform of each bank.

On the other hand, the level of security of credit or debit cards will depend on the level of security of the platform where the payments have been processed.

Because of this their security protocols, measures may not be effective enough because they may not follow global standards (each bank or payment system has its own standards).

4

PRESERVING THE VALUE OF YOUR MONEY WITH BITCOIN

HOW CAN BITCOIN HELP PRESERVE YOUR WEALTH?

F or most of Bitcoin's lifespan, the cryptocurrency and underlying blockchain has been used for mainly one purpose: investment. People put their money into the digital asset in the hope that it will increase exponentially in terms of fiat value.

Bitcoin has seen its fair share of price swings, and there have been many stories of people earning a lot of money when the price of bitcoin skyrockets. But there are other stories in which people have lost their life savings on a brutal downturn.

Peer-to-peer finance is taking a new course, and it has led to a flurry of new possibilities for Bitcoin users. These possibilities include making payments, sending remittances, and wealth preservation. As a matter of fact, there are several businesses accepting bitcoin already.

I will now cover some of the main features regarding Bitcoin as it pertains to locking in value:

1.) Bitcoin as a Means of Wealth Preservation

. . .

THE IDEA of using bitcoin as a means of wealth preservation can be done so in two ways: preserving your assets and preventing inflation on your currency.

2.) A Viable Money Reserve (Preserving Your Assets PYA)

FOR THOSE who are using bitcoin as a means of investment, rest assured to know that bitcoin is also a viable method for the preservation of wealth (PYA).

In many ways, bitcoin can be seen as the safest way to preserve your capital, for its limited supply and the technology of Blockchain make it safe and secure for all its users.

One of the biggest perks of using bitcoin is that it has no geographical borders, allowing you to send and receive bitcoin from anywhere in the world, anytime.

This means that traditional financial borders and barriers such as banks and other financial institutions will no longer be applicable—allowing you to have complete control over your money (assuming that you are in possession of your private keys).

Having a money reserve with bitcoin is something that a lot of people are starting to do in order to protect their assets as well as to have a backup plan in case of a financial disaster such as extreme inflation or oppression.

3.) Protecting the Value of Your Money (Eliminating Inflationary Risk)

IMAGINE THIS: your country is experiencing an extreme economic crisis, and the value of your currency is dropping rapidly. What's your way out?

To our comfort, a Venezuelan bitcoin holder learned that bitcoin has the power to save him and his family. Carlos Hernandez, a Ciudad Guayana native, now holds all his money in bitcoin and only withdraws small amounts when necessary.

As a country's economy can be volatile, and he could lose a lot of money when bolivars' value goes down, Carlos thinks that keeping his money all in bolivars is "financial suicide." This explains why he decided to convert all his assets into bitcoin wealth.

Bitcoin and cryptocurrency are usually seen as something "first world," but it's actually the developing countries (or countries with struggling economies like Venezuela) that have shown more openness in adopting them.

However, rather than using these digital assets as a means of investment—how a lot of bitcoin holders in developed countries use bitcoin—people in developing countries are using them as a means of survival.

A big portion of the world still remains unbanked (as of 2017), which basically means that they have the same financial rights as terrorists.

They're completely cut off from traditional financial services as they aren't allowed to trade or don't have access to any banking services they need.

This makes payments much harder for people who need them the most. On the other hand, bitcoin gives these people the financial passport and accessibility they really need, allowing them to gain access to affordable banking and the global free trade system.

As one of its real-use cases, bitcoin can be used as a means of wealth preservation for countries with struggling economies. Take Venezuela again as an example, their fiat currency is currently experiencing an inflation rate of 10 million percent (as of August 2019).

People are looking for a means of survival—and bitcoin comes in handy as their solution. Venezuelans have recently hit a bitcoin trading record of 120 billion bolivars as it's a very secure way for them to protect their fiat currency from experiencing any further hyperinflation.

4.) Gold vs. Bitcoin

GOLD AND BITCOIN are both extremely useful assets when it comes to the preservation of wealth. Gold is a precious metal and has long been a physical asset entailing unique properties such as rarity, durability, and beauty.

On the other hand, bitcoin is a relatively newly introduced digital asset with real-use cases that are yet to be discovered. Each of them has their own set of wealth preservation strategies.

In terms of security, gold and bitcoin are different in many ways. Gold is tangible and physical, allowing people to store it in whatever way they want.

Bitcoin, however, is digital, and if you lose access to your private keys, all can be lost within a matter of minutes—whether it be to hackers or just lost in general. On the other hand, gold can also be physically stolen, can erode, and the general quality of the gold can be tarnished.

Both assets have a limited supply, but gold has gone through thousands of years of competition with other forms of payment and secured its spot as the clear winner when it comes to the store of value. Because gold has been around for so long, people are more likely to believe in its value.

Bitcoin, on the other hand, despite having a limited supply as well, is believed to be potentially forked for more supply. Moreover, the price of bitcoin is volatile at times, and the prevention of money laundering/terrorist acts can hinder bitcoin from getting official support.

Nevertheless, with economic crises happening all over the world, bitcoin is just beginning to prove its real-life uses, and it's showing everyone that although it's not as respected as gold yet, it can be a viable means of wealth preservation.

5.) Why Bitcoin?

. . .

As YOU CAN SEE, the features of bitcoin evidently emancipate the unbanked from central control. Bitcoin, as a decentralized currency, provides people a means of traversing through the financial world without barriers.

In addition, bitcoin has the unique trait of being unable to be confiscated. This means that your bitcoin cannot be seized by any jurisdiction (as long as you own the private key).

Ask yourself this: which of the assets you own is non-confiscatable by a higher authority? The answer is that aside from bitcoin (and other cryptocurrencies), most assets are vulnerable to confiscation.

This makes bitcoin an ideal way to preserve your wealth, as well as to produce wealth. It's an asset that yo*au doesn't have to report.

Peer-to-peer finance is transforming the way bitcoin can be used. With more and more real-use cases, it's exciting to see bitcoin's capability to better societies and communities around the world—and it's only just the beginning.

5

THE PITFALLS AND MISTAKES PEOPLE MAKE WITH BITCOIN

WHAT ARE SOME COMMON MISTAKES PEOPLE MAKE WITH BITCOIN AND HOW TO PREVENT THEM?

W e've reached a point where good trading opportunities occur on a daily basis. With so many coins out there, it's impossible to be on top of all of them.

Well, let me tell you a secret, you don't have to be. You have to be patient and in control of your emotions. Some days you'll be sitting on your computer, looking at those hypnotizing green candles and big bull runs, and you'll want to trade so badly.

If you missed out on those trades, let them go. You can't enter such trades based just on the assumption that the bull-run will continue long enough for you to gain a portion of those profits. There's a big chance that your impatience will cost you dearly. It often happens that you buy at the top and face a big drop in price afterward.

Entering in a hasty trade without a clear strategy is a terrible idea. But if you put in some effort and learn how to analyze the coin/chart, set up an entry, exit, and target points and adjust position size correctly, you will be able to know the difference between a good and a bad trade.

Your goal must always be to pick the best possible trade. And remember a good trader always trades less. The cryptocurrency market is booming, and it will continue to do so.

What started in 2009 can't be undone. More and more people are learning about cryptocurrencies and are thinking about investing in them.

They ask me questions like... Is bitcoin going to rise even more? Should I invest some money in there? Which cryptocurrency is the best?

My answer usually goes something like this: trading in the cryptocurrency market has been extremely profitable so far.

It seems like our group has made the right moves. We got really good at spotting potential profits and taking advantage of them.

Of course, sometimes things don't turn out as expected, but we know the risks, and we know how to minimize them. Trading nowadays seems simple, because we have the knowledge and the experience.

In order to make your life a little easier, especially for beginners, I listed some of the topics, you have to take into consideration before you start trading:

1. Don't Let Your Bitcoin Out of Your Sight

Bitcoin is an essential part of cryptocurrencies. You must

always know what BTC is doing. Is it in a consolidation state, a bull run, or in a bear run?

What's the latest news that might influence sudden price change or a trend reversal? This is important because you'll be mostly trading with an altcoin/bitcoin pair.

You'll have to keep an eye on both currencies. There's a general rule that when bitcoin's price is rising, all other currencies will be in red numbers. And when bitcoin's price decreases, alts will be back in the green.

There are exceptions where you will profit from both bitcoin and altcoin going up, but don't get caught in the opposite scenario where you'll get slammed.

When you're not sure what to expect, trade with the good old altcoin/fiat currency pair. The only downside is that there are not as many options on the table.

THE MOST IMPORTANT advice I have to offer in this entire book is the famous quote below:

.   .   .

"IF YOU DON'T HOLD the private keys to your bitcoin, it's not your bitcoin."

OR A SHORTER VERSION OF THIS, "not your keys, then they're not your bitcoins."

IF YOU THINK your bitcoins are safe in an exchange or being held by a third party, think again. A common way to think about bitcoins is to think about controlling rights. You never truly hold a bitcoin, but you can hold a key to control its movement.

That control of a bitcoin's movement is the closest thing you will ever get to ownership of it. Sure we have the ability to move money from our bank to another bank, until they decided to arbitrarily freeze our account for no reason.

In this sense Bitcoin is a lot more real than your bank account balance is or ever has been. If you and only you hold the keys, nobody can take that Bitcoin away from you. How's that for digital financial freedom?

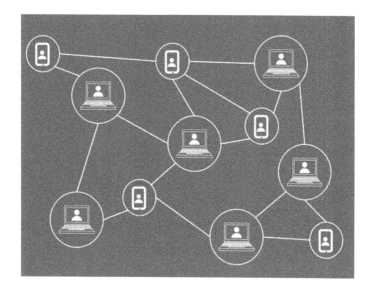

2. Volatility Has to Work for You, Not Against You

THIS MARKET IS so volatile that sometimes you'll get shivers from it. The huge swings in price are usually a result of large investors buying and selling. These investors are referred to as whales in cryptocurrency lingo. Whales' moves, pump & dump, and FOMO events are big contributors to overall volatility in the Bitcoin market. But on the other hand, T=the volatility can work both ways.

It can make you rich, or it can leave you penniless if you are foolish. It's worth mentioning also that some exchanges offer margin trading as well. I strongly recommend that you stay away from it if you are new to trading. Keep in mind that things can change very quickly.

3. Practice with a Small Trading Position Size and Master the Exchange

IF YOU JUST STARTED TRADING, your position size should be small. Why? Well, because you have to be 100% sure of what you are doing when you want to execute a specific order.

You have to know your way around the exchange that you are trading on. Write things down if needed. When the time comes for you to place orders, you will have to act *q*quickly. There will be no room for errors. Place small incremental buy and sell orders, stop-loss orders, and practice as much as needed.

If you master one exchange, it doesn't mean you know them all. When you trade on five or more exchanges, you will notice that they differ in many ways.

Before choosing an exchange, always check the following characteristics: fees, liquidity, security, option for short/option for margin trading, and other features.

4. Only Enter a Trade When You Have a Clear Strategy

I MENTIONED A FEW THINGS ALREADY, but going in a trade blind is a no-go. Maybe you'll get lucky a couple of times, but in the long run, you don't stand a chance. In order to achieve success, you have to combine fundamental and technical analysis.

You have to stick to your strategy, no matter what. Once you enter a trade with calculated position size, you will know how much risk are you willing to take and where you will take your profit.

.   .   .

5. Adapt, Analyze Trades and Learn From Your Mistakes

TRADERS WHO DON'T ANALYZE their trading performance are more prone to make repetitive mistakes. As a trader, you must constantly improve in order to survive and thrive in this fast-paced market. This is a vital part of trading.

There's lots of room for improvement, even if you are an experienced trader. Try to be on top of all major global cryptocurrency market events. Adapt and try to learn from them and avoid unnecessary risks. When opportunity comes knocking, take advantage of them and secure easy profits.

6. Have Your Own Opinion

UNFORTUNATELY, the unregulated environment of cryptocurrencies has attracted the attention of scammers. Do your own research.

Don't trust the guy with a free ticket to the moon

in the forum. Check different social channels, blogs, forums, news, and review sites and see for yourself if the project that you are about to invest in is credible.

This is especially relevant for ICO's and the early adoption of investment trading strategies. In the end, it is you who sends the money away.

Ask yourself, can I afford to lose this money? I recommend that you evaluate the situation carefully before jumping into uncharted waters.

7. Control your emotions

EASIER SAID THAN DONE. Emotions are a constant unwanted companion in trading. It's easy to get carried away by greed, fear, hope, or excitement, among everything else.

Different situations will bring different emotions, and it is up to you how you will handle them. When you have a bad trade, the negativity surrounding the outcome can carry over into the next trade.

It may happen that you won't enter your next trade due to the fear of losing. On the contrary, when you have a winning streak, you might think you're invincible and push trades into the market at the wrong time.

Boredom or the need to trade can easily cloud your judgment and cause you to enter a trade when you shouldn't. Before entering a trade, it always helps to ask yourself for the reasons behind the actions that you're about to take.

Practice resilience. Rather than letting the fear of losing, greed, failure, and stress overwhelm you, use them as learning experiences and stepping stones to becoming a better trader.

6

THE DIFFERENCE BETWEEN BLOCKCHAIN, BITCOIN AND OTHER CRYPTOCURRENCIES

1. WHAT EXACTLY DO THEY MEAN WHEN THEY SAY BLOCKCHAIN TECHNOLOGY?

2. WHAT IS THE DIFFERENCE BETWEEN BLOCKCHAINS AND DIGITAL CURRENCIES?

Part of the confusion around what is blockchain versus what is cryptocurrency is due in part to the fact that the terms have come into use incorrectly and without regard to their proper usage. Instead of being introduced by formal definition, the term blockchain developed from a "chain of blocks."

Cryptocurrency is a sort of portmanteau of

"cryptographic currency." But the fundamental difference between these concepts has to do with how distributed ledger technology is used.

KEEP READING for a clearer idea of the difference between blockchains and cryptocurrencies.

1. Blockchain As A Technology

When Bitcoin was the first and only digital asset and it also operated the only blockchain network, there wasn't much of a distinction between the terms, and they were used interchangeably.

As the technology matured and a variety of blockchains bloomed, the uses quickly diverged from the pure money aspect. Instead, technologists experimented with ideas such as a decentralized name registry.

Other uses utilized the peer-to-peer aspect to deliver messages in a private manner. In the end, many of these projects failed to find good uses of technology. The projects left standing helped demonstrate what was possible beyond buzzwords.

A blockchain is a distributed ledger technology that forms a "chain of blocks." Each block includes information and data that are bundled together and verified.

These blocks are then validated and strung onto the chain of transactions and information in previous blocks.

These blocks of transactions are permanently recorded in the distributed ledger that is the blockchain. Learn more about blockchain technology here.

One of the greatest benefits to running transactions on a highly decentralized blockchain is the transparency it presents to users. Combine that with the programmed consistency regarding inflationary methods and you truly have a superior store of value when compared to fiat currencies.

. . .

2. Cryptocurrency as an Asset Class

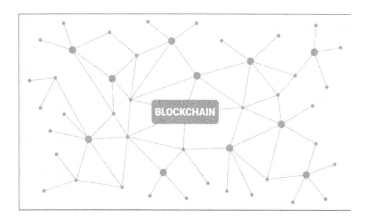

In contrast with blockchain, cryptocurrency is to do with the use of tokens based on the distributed ledger technology. Cryptocurrency can be seen as a tool or resource on a blockchain network.

Anything dealing with buying, selling, investing, trading, microtipping, or other monetary aspects, deals with a blockchain native token or subtoken.

It is a token based on the distributed ledger that is a blockchain. Cryptocurrency is a digital currency formed on the basis of cryptography, or by definition: "the art of solving mathematical equations."

Referring to the token as the technology can be correct in the case of Bitcoin, but it is very different when dealing with other blockchain projects such as

Ethereum. In this case, the technology is known as Ethereum, but the native token is Ether, and transactions are paid in a small percentage of ETH referred to as 'gas.'

How Cryptocurrencies and Blockchain Compliment Each Other

Blockchain is the platform that brings cryptocurrencies into play—it is the technology that serves as the distributed ledger that forms the network. This network creates the means for transacting and enables transferring of value and information.

Cryptocurrencies are the tokens used within these networks and can be used to transfer value and settle outstanding debts.

Furthermore, you can see them as a tool on a blockchain, in some cases serving as a resource or utility function. Other times they are used for digitizing the value of an asset.

Blockchains serve as the basis technology in which cryptocurrencies operate on top of, facilitating a cryptocurrency's ecosystem.

7

TIPS AND TRICKS FOR TRADING BITCOIN AND OTHER CRYPTOCURRENCIES

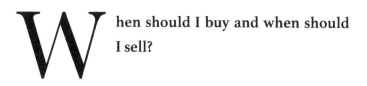

W
hen should I buy and when should I sell?

"WHEN IS THE best time to buy/sell assets in the cryptocurrency market?"—That's the million-dollar question lingering in the back of every crypto trader's mind.

Much like trading traditional assets and commodities, it pays to observe the price movements of virtual coins. Market timing is a debatable subject when it comes to trading strategies. Some traders are for it, while there are those that claim it's impossible.

In a nutshell, market timing is a buying/selling trading strategy built upon the concept of beating the market by predicting its price fluctuations. The projections dive into technical and fundamental analyses to assess the market and economic conditions.

If the investor accurately predicts price movements, they can move their assets quickly and turn them into profit. A lot of crypto traders and investors use their own custom strategies to predict which virtual coins are set to rise or tank.

WHY IS THE Market Timing Strategy Effective in Crypto Investing?

CRYPTOCURRENCY MARKETS ARE relatively new and as such can take quite a bit of time to get your head wrapped around. The market comes with risks due to the volatile nature of the industry in general.

But where there is risk, there may also be reward and markets can provide exceptional opportunities for gains. With this in mind, a lot of existing and aspiring investors are basing their buying decisions on market timing. But, how does this strategy hold water in the cryptospace?

From choosing to take distributions from your 401(k), to selling your rental property because you couldn't find replacement tenants, every investment decision you make is tied in with market timing to an extent.

Cryptocurrencies are traded 24 hours a day, all around the world. It is a market that never closes, which makes it all the more important to pay attention to price movements.

With its volatile market, understanding it and assessing your risk tolerance is a vital step before buying any investments. Knowing the security of your assets, price history and recurring patterns helps you to come up with an educated guess.

The more you understand how the market works, the more you're inclined you may be to take a higher risk in your investment decisions which may also result in higher returns.

When to Buy and When to Sell

If you want an honest answer, the best time to

invest in crypto was yesterday, but the second best time could be right now. Just take a look at the price history of Bitcoin.

If you'd paid attention to it when it was still new and bought a "minimal amount" of BTC, you'd be a millionaire today.

But since we're dealing with the present, here are a few tips to help you decide when the perfect time to buy and sell is:

Use the "Buy Low, Sell High" Strategy

Otherwise phrased as "buy the dips," this basic investment technique refers to purchasing more assets as the price falls and/or once it settles.

This move is best recommended to use in a stagnant or bull market where the usual trend is rising or sideways, rather than in a bear market where the general direction is downwards.

The logic of the "BTD" strategy involves analyzing charts, short-term and long-term average movements, historical support trends, and laddering buys. Investors can buy "big dips" or "little dips."

The former refers to when the price drops below

average, while the latter refers to when the price falls from wherever it placed last. People who buy dips can choose to sell fast for a profit, hold on to it to build a long-term position or use it to incrementally take gains.

The bottom line—the crux of the strategy is to buy at a lower price, not a higher one. Doing so gives you less room for big mistakes.

While purchasing a dipping asset is an ideal strategy, it's hard to tell how the price will perform in the next hour, following day, etc.

Educated guesses based on analysis can only give you so much information. Meanwhile, there's another way you can consider entering the market: when the price of a famed virtual coin rates lower than its average historical projection.

Many cryptocurrency websites provide moving average charts that illustrate the best possible points to enter and exit the crypto market.

However it should be made clear that charts can vary from site to site so you may want to check a few to get a general idea of averages.

Don't buy when the price is peaking. Instead, wait for it to settle and purchase after the sell-off point.

. . .

SELL WHEN THERE'S a Sudden Peak

WHEN IT COMES to selling your coins, you need to consider your finances, risk tolerance, tax consequences, and the reason why you initially invested in crypto.

Yale researchers studied the price movements of major cryptocurrencies and found that the best risk-free time for trading digital assets is the following week in which the price encountered a sudden increase of more than 20%, they recommend that the week following this increase is either a great time to sell or buy but it will depend on market factors and technical analysis to figure out the appropriate action to take.

WHEN TO NOT BUY OR Sell

WHEN BUYING CRYPTOCURRENCIES, you should watch and study the price movements closely before you take action. The same goes for selling—don't rush and jump into selling only to expose your coins to the potential of significant losses.

. . .

Avoiding the Common FOMO (Fear of Missing Out)

Indeed, it's hard to watch Bitcoin, Ripple or other coins peaking like crazy in just a few minutes. People flooding trading groups, Reddit, Telegram and other discussion groups to talk about the rise is even harder to watch as an outsider.

However, you shouldn't let this fear of missing out trigger you to act impulsively (buying the top coins, panic selling the bottom) and join the bandwagon.

Missing out on big activities often causes beginner traders and investors to immaturely buy an asset so as not to miss out on a presumed opportunity. The best way to avoid this situation is to shrug off the noise and base your investment decisions on logic, not emotion.

When You Don't Understand the Technology

. . .

WHAT MAKES cryptocurrencies highly innovative and forthcoming is their primal technology—blockchain. When you start investing in virtual coins, you can't rely on other people to dictate what moves you should make next.

If you don't have a firm grasp of the foundations and workarounds of the technology yet, do more research first. Otherwise, jumping head-first into things will be much riskier.

Once you understand what consensus algorithms, block rewards, premining, on-chain/off-chain, and what all the other jargon used in the industry means, you'll have a better grasp of the industry in whole and where the biggest opportunities are to be found.

Soon, you'll know when you're ready to penetrate the market as a knowledgeable investor.

WHEN YOU'RE Vulnerable to FUD (Fear, Uncertainty, and Doubt)

THE GOAL OF FUD is to encourage you to sell, not to buy. For instance, when scammers want to purchase a coin at a lower price, they will intentionally spread negative news about hacking, security issues, and other aspects to destabilize a challenging market and get other traders and investors to panic sell.

Knowing that the crypto market is volatile makes it easy for FUDsters to manipulate the market and start a pump and dump scheme—having investors "dump" their assets with the risk of losses, giving FUDsters the opportunity to catch the dumped digital assets at a low market price.

Again, the best thing to do when you sense this happening is to use logic. You bought the assets for a reason. Get behind the motives around this scenario and don't act on impulse.

8

INTERESTING FACTS RELATED TO BITCOIN

The financial world can be a confusing place full of strange terms, unusual forms of currency, and endless trading options.

Unfortunately for those who are not so tech-savvy, the integration of the internet into our daily lives has allowed the financial world to evolve.

In addition to extensive banking, payment, and stock options that have become the norm online, there are also new currencies that have been created.

These cryptocurrencies—digital currencies with encryptions to maintain security and validity—feature real value, and can be exchanged for USD,

GBP, or any other type of physical currency through online options.

The most popular type of virtual currency is known as Bitcoin and has steadily begun to rise in popularity and strength over the years.

At first glance, Bitcoin may look confusing, however, below are ten facts that will truly explain in layman's terms what exactly Bitcoin is and how it came to be.

No Single Entity Controls Bitcoin

Confusing? Yeah, most people think so too at first. The general concept of currency and money is that a bank controls it, that there are rises and falls in its value based on the global market, and that you can physically hold it.

Bitcoin, is controlled by everyone who uses it as the blockchain software that underpins the currency logs and validates activities that have taken place on the bitcoin blockchain all across the globe.

There's a Finite Number of Bitcoins

· · ·

You would think that because there's no need to physically print the bills or mint the coins that there would be an infinite number of bitcoins in existence. However, that would devalue the currency and render it worthless. Instead, there are exactly 21,000,000 coins.

Bitcoins Have No Inherent or Set Value

If you look at a dollar bill, you know that it is simply a piece of paper with a number on it and some fancy pictures saying that it is worth $1.00. It, in fact, only has value because we say it does.

Bitcoin always stays the same while the value in FIAT terms is in constant flux.

Those little digital pieces of code are only worth money because people say they are and they then trade real goods/services for them. The more popular Bitcoin gets, the more value is going to be placed on each individual bitcoin.

· · ·

You Can See All Transactions

The uni' ue thing about Bitcoin is that it is completely transparent. Not with personal data, no, but instead with transactions and amounts.

Everything can be easily identified on a blockchain, and it's because of this complete transparency that Bitcoin has become a much more trusted digital asset.

An open ledger that is accessible by anyone in the world creates a 'trustless' environment which can facilitate a level of comfort with an asset class that is almost nowhere to be found when compared to traditional institutional assets.

You Can Mine Bitcoins

Mining bitcoins is a term that refers to someone using a computer program to solve mathematical problems to verify various transactions around the world.

Bitcoin miners then get paid a certain number of bitcoins for solving those problems.

· · ·

No Transaction Reversals, No Claims on Your Bitcoins

ONE OF THE most integral features of bitcoins are that you can never be forced to pay, but nor can you take back a transaction once you have paid meaning you cannot revoke transactions.. Companies and individuals also cannot repeat bill you and force money to be taken out.

You Can Send Money With Little to No Fees

IF YOU WANT to send money to a friend in Thailand and you are in the United Kingdom, you'd likely have to pay bank transfer fees, currency conversion fees, and more.

Additionally, your friend may have to wait a few days before the money becomes available.

With bitcoins, there are little to no transaction fees, and the money is available almost instantly.

· · ·

Bitcoins Are Held in Digital Wallets

Much like when you log into your online bank account and see your balance, you get an online Bitcoin wallet that is established when you sign up. This wallet is like a physical wallet, but much more secure.

If you lose it, it's lost forever; however, it's impossible for people to take money from your wallet without you giving it to them.

Additionally, if you know a Bitcoin address, you can see how many bitcoins they have and vice versa.

Losing a Wallet Means Bitcoins Are Lost Forever (Deflationary)

While the bitcoins in the wallet may still be in existence because they were recorded on the blockchain, they are no longer able to be spent if the wallet is lost.

These bitcoins have unique keys to them, and so if they're lost with a wallet, then they are essentially removed from circulation forever.

. . .

You Can Really Buy Things with Bitcoins

Bitcoins may sound a bit farcical at first, but they're actually a real currency used to buy real things.

There are a variety of merchants who accept bitcoins as payment for items, both online and in person.

Popular online stores that accept bitcoins include Newegg, Overstock, Microsoft and Dell.

Physical stores include Reeds Jewelers, One Shot Hotels, Holiday Inn (located in New York), and even local pizza places and restaurants.

You can even use bitcoins to gamble, buy gold bullion, or donate to charity.

9

INVESTING IN BITCOIN AND DIGITAL ASSETS

HOW TO BECOME SUCCESSFUL INVESTING IN BITCOIN AND OTHER DIGITAL ASSETS

D
o you believe Bitcoin and other cryptocurrencies are ready to skyrocket again?

Since its inception in 2010, Bitcoin was the first digital asset to beget an entire ecosystem of cryptocurrencies. For quite some time, it had a growing underground following of investors who seemed very interested in its future as a possible replacement to the physical monetary system, as traditional institutional players curiously watched its development.

While we are still likely many years away from a complete transition, the crypto space has been a fairly volatile playground.

During the ascension and adoption of crypto, many people launched ICOs (Individual Coin Offerings, akin to offering a new stock) without any supervision or regulation. This is a topic that I will go into more in a future title. If you aren't aware of ICO's an the difference between an ICO and an IPO, there are plenty of resources readily available on the web that can go over the basic differences between the two.

In this most recent phase, Bitcoin led the charge to a valuation of nearly $20,000 per coin in 2017, but then its value steadily declined over the course of 2018 and settled in the range of $3,500 to $4,000 for quite some time.

After witnessing the meteoric rise and subsequent fall of Bitcoin's value, many folks became gun-shy about investing in cryptocurrencies. This has steadily changed over the past couple of years, as the crypto market has matured due to more oversight and regulatory controls put in place by institutions and government agencies.

As a result of these measures and the increase of institutional dollars supporting the industry, more people are now seeking ways to invest in Bitcoin while at the same time being cautious as to not invest more than they can afford to lose due to Bitcoin's volatile nature.

SUCESSFUL CRYPTOCURRENCY INVESTING Advice From Industry Experts

1. Diversify Your Risk When Investing in Bitcoin and Cryptocurrencies

IN TODAY'S "INSTANT GRATIFICATION" oriented society, many people are guilty of trying totime the crypto market and win big, almost with a "win-the-lottery" type of mentality.

However, Parul Gujral says this is a recipe for probable disaster. In my video interview with the

CEO of Snowball, Gujral agrees that you can still win big if you time the market just right, but as many people experienced in 2018, you can also lose big just as quickly.

He believes the key to success when it comes to investing in cryptocurrencies is to diversify your risk by investing in a pool of cryptocurrencies that are vetted by financial professionals, just like your 401k accounts or index funds.

"With our mobile app, we let you invest in cryptocurrencies or digital assets like Warren Buffet wants you to invest in stocks through the S&P 500. Warren Buffett, Ray Dalio, and even Tony Robbins in his book *Money Master the Game*, all recommend index investing. By investing in an index, the fees and risks are much lower, it's tax-optimized, and you can typically outperform the market," Gujral said.

The recommendation of investing in an index fund means you're not putting "all your eggs in one basket" like many people did when they invested in a single coin or ICO and lost big when the cryptocurrency market deflated in 2018.

Paul Veradittakit, a partner at Pantera Capital, also recommends the concept of diversifying cryptocurrency investments: "I think if you're an individual investor, it makes sense to try to diversify as much as possible just because there is a lot of risk in cryptocurrency and a lot of volatility, and you want to make sure that you have a basket of them and hopefully hit on one of the investments that will do very well."

However, most people only have access to invest in crypto funds or indices if they are an accredited investor—someone who makes over $200,000 for 2+ consecutive years and/or has $1 million of assets, not counting primary real estate. This means the novice or average person typically doesn't have the ability to invest in a crypto fund.

It's a major reason why Gujral founded Snowball and hopes his app will help democratize access to the best crypto fund and index strategies. He believes the average investor should be able to wisely invest in the cryptocurrency sector with less friction and reduced risk.

2. Invest Through Regulated Professionals

ANOTHER CHALLENGE IS FINDING those financial professionals who can effectively research and recommend a portfolio of cryptos that provide a steady return on investment (ROI), while minimizing your exposure to a bear—or down—market.

There are a plethora of options when it comes to cryptocurrency apps and investment platforms, but one of the differentiating factors investors should seek when working with financial professionals are choosing those who have earned Registered Investment Advisor (RIA) status by the Securities Exchange Commission.

According to Investopedia, "RIAs have a fiduciary duty to their clients, which means they have a fundamental obligation to provide investment advice that always acts in their clients' best interests. As the first word of their title indicates, RIAs are required to register either with the Securities and Exchange Commission (SEC) or state securities administrators."

This designation essentially means that RIAs are not only regulated, but are also fiscally responsible for their investment advice and recommendations.

"We've become a registered investment advisor or an RIA, just like Andreessen Horowitz announced they require all of their firms to have registered investment advisors," said Gujral.

"Since we are managing people's money and

digital assets, we felt like it was extremely important to 1) have a stamp of approval stating that we're qualified and then 2) have a set of eyes regulating us. So now we're regulated by the SEC and FINRA, and at some juncture in the horizon, we will also be regulated by FinCEN, but not yet."

During an interview with Veradittakit, whose investment firm has funded over 100 crypto-related projects, I asked how important the RIA designation is for the future of the industry.

"I think it's a big deal. I think it's good that investors and entrepreneurs do whatever they can to protect themselves with regulations. When you are managing other folks' money, becoming an RIA with the SEC is a great way to provide credibility and have the right licensing to do what you want to do across asset management. It's why Pantera became an RIA as well."

As the cryptocurrency ecosystem continues to evolve and become more complex, it will only become time-consuming and challenging to know which coins and tokens are worth betting on and which ones to avoid. Working with registered professionals may help to save time and hopefully increase your odds of a profitable investment.

A worthwhile resource is the SEC investor

bulletins which provide a list of tips and questions to ask before selecting a financial professional.

3. Focus on Education and Wealth Accumulation

REGARDLESS, it's not wise to ignorantly entrust your capital to any financial advisor, app or crypto company without doing any of your own due diligence and research. After all, you're ultimately responsible for the outcome of your decision.

Gujral recommended Coinbase Earn as a good place to start for education. According to their site, Coinbase offers to pay people to learn about cryptocurrencies through completing educational tasks like watching short video lessons and completing quizzes.

Their organization is a regulated broker-dealer and, according to Gujral, they've received their RIA designation from the SEC as well.

During an interview with Gordy Bal, the CEO of Conscious Thought Revolution, who has invested in companies like Bulletproof Coffee and WAX, I asked why people should educate themselves on the industry.

He replied, "Over the next 25 years, Accenture reports there will be a wealth transfer of over $30 trillion in North America, moving from baby boomers to their heirs, and it will be the greatest wealth transfer in history.

There is no question if cryptocurrency is going to be a thing. It's just an inevitability. I think what would serve people really well is to understand the underlying technology from a philosophical standpoint and how it can serve a greater purpose."

While some folks are willing to bet big by day trading and timing the markets, the average and novice investors may not want to expose themselves to significant risks and potential losses, and may want to adopt a more conservative approach.

As per Veradittakit, "If you have the time and you have the skill set to actively day trade, and you can do well at it, then go for it. But I think for most folks, they're just not going to have that skill set or the time. I think the biggest thing is really finding projects or companies that you're passionate about and invest in a portfolio of cryptocurrencies for the long term."

Bal concurs, "I would say, instead of focusing on the possibility of making massive amounts of returns, make it about aligning with a project that speaks for the future of our race, our species and our planet. Focus on the long game—find the founders who have a mission, who have had multiple successes before, and who are already being funded by the Andreessens of the world. Play alongside them by investing in these deals."

With major financial institutions and corporations like JP Morgan, USAA, Goldman Sachs and IBM backing crypto, as well as Facebook's recent announcement of their own coin, it seems that cryptocurrencies are here to stay. In fact, Gujral is so bullish on the future of crypto that he plans to have Snowball be amongst the first to integrate with Facebook's Libra coin.

In an email, sent to a client, Reese Jones—a venture strategist who serves as an advisor to both Facebook and Snowball—stated, "Facebook's Libra will introduce upwards of a billion people to digital crypto money payments, and many of those people will, of course, want to diversify their money investments into portfolios as facilitated by Snowball."

As the industry continues to mature and grow, it may be wise to research and learn how to invest in the crypto markets intelligently. Investing in your financial education is usually profitable, and a conservative cryptocurrency strategy could pay big dividends in the long run.

Even Yale suggests that investors should put up to six percent of their assets into cryptocurrencies.

"Remember when your Gmail name was taken because you took too long to get your Gmail address? It's the same thing with investing in cryptocurrency."

These are the moments that you can get in at an early stage, like you would have been able to for the Googles and Amazons in the early 2000s.

Just get in the game, whatever that looks like. Don't be so behind the curve, where a few years down the road, you reflect and wish you took action."

AFTERWORD

Investing in Bitcoin and other cryptocurrencies is certainly risky due to their subjective underlying value and high volatility. But, oddly, these same traits are actually bringing many people into the market.

Another thing that Bitcoin investors like is the fact that many of them got in on the ground floor. This means that they're early adopters and have less to lose, perhaps because their initial investment may have been much smaller.

Sure, BTC has been around since 2009, but many of the altcoins (substitutes for Bitcoin or completely different cryptocurrencies altogether) are new.

They offer people a chance to get in on the ground floor, but the ground floor of what? You may see your money fall through the floor, so the risk may not be worth the potential reward in many cases.

Without a doubt, Bitcoin has made millionaires and brought unimaginable wealth to the people who believed in it, purchased it and held on to it. But many others just want to know, when we will see the next Bitcoin?

Will there ever be another financial opportunity like the one we have just missed in our lifetimes? Numerous investors are now simply taking wild shots at digital assets they believe could compete or compliment Bitcoin, and they are putting money into projects when they are still untested and in their infancy. This may have worked with Bitcoin but back then, it was the only cryptocurrency!

Regardless of the points mentioned above, if you really want to avoid the three common mistakes and end up effectively prospering from the blockchain revolution, remember these important tips:

• Avoid investing more than you can afford to lose.

• Don't fall victim to FOMO (Fear of missing out).

• Look for long-term value.

Above all, don't be convinced that you must buy right away or you'll miss out. We're still very early in the cryptocurrency revolution, meaning that you still have plenty of time to research projects and make the right decisions when it comes to investing.

I sinercely hope this guide can act as a key to a better life through the understanding and active use of cryptocurrencies. I'd just like to say one last thing before we part ways; that thing relates to teamwork.

I can confidently say, beyond a doubt, that this new world of digital assets and decentralized networks has the power to change things for the better, if we can come together and direct its path appropriately.

Together, we can bring about a new, more transparent age of wealth and value exchange. Blockchain technologies like Bitcoin can help us bring that age about.

Thank you for taking the time to read this guide and good luck in applying your newfound knowledge of cryptocurrencies.

Sincerely,

Marc Gordon

ABOUT THE AUTHOR

Marc Gordon is a human rights activist, computer programmer and cryptocurrency expert. Beyond that he prides himself on being able to explain complex concepts like Bitcoin, blockchain and distributed ledger technology to the masses.

In a new age, a digital currency revolution is taking place and it's something we have never seen before. It will transform the world as we know it and become the new way in which value transactions primarily take place.

Marc Gordon's passion for creating high quality non-fiction titles about cryptocurrencies and technology is undeniable and he will continue to deliver world class titles to his beloved readers.

Do Not Go Yet; One Last Thing To Do

If you enjoyed this book or found it useful, I'd be very grateful if you'd post a short review on Amazon. Your support really does make a difference, and I read all the reviews personally so I can get your feedback and make this book even better.

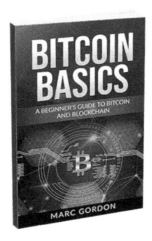

Click Here to Leave a Review on Amazon.com

Thanks again for your support!

ADVISE AUTHOR PUBLISHING

Please take a moment to review some of the other amazing titles by Advise Author Publishing now available in the Amazon Kindle store:

1.) The Snake That Ate Its Own Tail: A Short Story From Dystopity

Micah Jovich, a veteran mercenary and brilliant computer scientist and programmer takes charge of the Transition, an interstellar battleship with the help of his trusty android and protector Debian.

Micah and Debian along with the help of Diah-sees give it their all to deliver the final finishing blow to the Syndicate and wrestle back independent control of Tremaine's little corner of the quadrant. <u>As if anything were ever that easy, the ruthless chief occupation officer of the Syndicate, Trilian Six, expertly captures Micah sending all their plans into a tailspin.</u>

Debian and Diahsees are placed in a difficult situation and forced to use every single trick in the book to save Micah his creator and restore freedom to the citizens of Tremaine. <u>The entire future of the galaxy rests in their hands as they desperately try to save Micah and restore balance to the quadrant.</u>

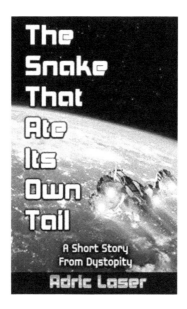

2.) The Beginner's Guide to Blogging: 25 Essential Tips For Turning Your Blogging Passion Into Profits

Have you noticed how some bloggers make six or seven-figure incomes while others struggle to even make $100? What if I could teach you some key skills and habits that could make your blog a true success financially?

One of the biggest secrets I can share about blogging, one that I quickly came to understand from other successful communicators, is that you have to be **passionate** about what you're writing. But this book has so much more to offer.

In this book, you'll find easy step-by-step instructions on how to:

* Setup your very own blog.
  * Analyze and select a specific niche that is both profitable and that you are passionate about.
  * Promote and market your blog using several proven social media marketing strategies.
  * Apply basic content strategy and design elements to your blog posts to make them go viral.
  * Apply 25 essential blogging tips that can help you turn passion into profit.

While you may not get instantly rich from blogging it is something you can easily build upon in your spare time and expand into a full-fledged career path. In this book you will learn everything you need to know to get a huge advantage in blogging by standing on the shoulders of some of the most successful bloggers ever to put words on a page.

For less than a cup of coffee, this book will literally

teach you how to turn your <u>passion into profit</u>, <u>become your own boss</u> and eventually <u>leave the day job behind</u>!

3.) She Gets It Done: How Successful Women Manage Their Time

In **She Gets It Done**™ you will learn:

✓ How to transform yourself into an extremely productive person.

✓ Tips and tricks that will show you how to work smarter, not harder.

✓ How to free up massive amounts of time by looking at the big picture and delegating tasks.

✓ How to organize your time in a more logical and efficient way, leaving more time for you.

✓ How to prioritize your most important tasks and eliminate wasted time on the things that simply don't matter much.

Do you think it's impossible to find the time to do things that make you happy? Think again because, I've done it and now I want to show you how!

There's no time to wait. The clock is ticking and we need to make the most of it. Grab a copy of this book and let me show you how to really make the most from your time!

Sincerely,

♥ Tina Stokes

4.) 25 Natural Soap Recipes: A Beginner's Guide for Making All Natural Soap Bars at Home

Did you know that many store bought soaps contain toxic chemicals and ingredients that really shouldn't be allowed in them?

This brand new step-by-step beginners guide will teach you everything you need to know about making all natural soaps at home. The easy to follow instructions will walk you through each stage.

♥ *Wouldn't it be great to ditch the store bought soaps and replace them with all natural handmade organic soap bars?*

If you love to make handmade gifts, you're really going to love this new all natural soap making book so if you're ready to make some all natural soaps, this book can help you get started:

25 Natural Soap Recipes: The Best Beginner's DIY Guide for Making All Natural Organic Home-made Soap Bars at Home.

5.) Herbal Medicine for Everyone: The Beginner's Guide to Healing Common Illnesses with 20 Medicinal Herbs

Herbal Medicine for Everyone™ is the go to guide for alleviating common illnesses through the use of over 20 medicinal herbs.

The number of handbooks and guides covering this topic can make finding the right book extremely overwhelming.

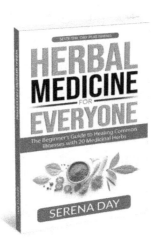

✓ Fortunately, it doesn't take a genius to begin harnessing the power of herbal medicine to cure common illnesses, it only takes some basic training and initiative.

Herbal Medicine for Everyone highlights effective herbs and homemade remedies that assist in the body's natural ability to fight off infections and ultimately cure itself of the common illnesses that plague us frequently.

<u>This book will transform readers into junior herbalists who can easily recognize the most abundant and effective medicinal herbs that they can use to craft powerful remedies for common illnesses.</u>

★ Included are remedies proven to be effective in reducing the severity of headaches, fevers, allergies and many other common ailments. Junior herbalists will learn the essential knowledge they need to transform into highly skilled naturopathic caregivers and gain a unique ability to apply herbal medicine effectively.

Herbal Medicine for Everyone teaches you how to use herbs as preventative and restorative medicine with:

✓ An Herbal Medicine Orientation provides the building blocks of knowledge when it comes to purchasing, making, and using herbal medicine in an effective manner.

 ✓ An Overview of Popular Herbs teaches you how to select the appropriate herbs for your medicinal herbal pantry.

 ✓ 20+ Herbal Remedies for Common Ailments with step-by-step instructions on how to make them in the comfort of your own home.

You'll learn how to alleviate stress with linden, soothe and comfort burns using marshmallow and detoxify your body using dandelion.

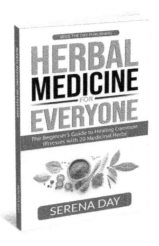

Get a copy of "Herbal Medicine for Everyone" today and ditch the store bought meds forever.